S0-ARM-719

PROPERTY OF

COMMONWEALTH OF PENNSYLVANIA

ESEA TITLE II, 1973

For their help in the preparation of this book, grateful acknowledgment is made to Victor Hugo-Vidal, Jr., President, Cedar Lodge Farm, Stamford, Connecticut; to Joseph Schmidt, Instructor, Cedar Lodge Farm; and to Sandy Johnson and Teri Ardleigh, both of Greenwich, Connecticut, who served as photographic models. Special thanks are also offered A. L. Waintrob of Budd Studio, New York City, whose distinctive photographs appear throughout the book.

The author also wishes to give credit for the following photographs: Roosevelt Raceway, page 12; New York Racing Association (Bob Coglianese), page 12; Miller's, page 18; and H. Kauffman & Sons, pages 17 and 53.

BETTER HORSEBACK RIDING
for Boys and Girls

George Sullivan

Rockwood Area Elementary
School Library

DODD, MEAD & COMPANY · NEW YORK

ACCESSION NO. 3169

FEB 4 1974

Copyright © 1969 by George Sullivan

All rights reserved

No part of this book may be reproduced in any form

without permission in writing from the publisher

Library of Congress Catalog Card Number: 75-88071

Printed in the United States of America

FOREWORD

When I was a child, I never owned a horse of my own, and as a result I used to read anything "horsey" that I could get my hands on, always hoping to find words of wisdom and sage advice—any shortcut to riding success. After many, many books and magazine articles, I realized two things: that the horse is the best teacher of all, and that perfection is never really attainable, but must always be striven for through patience and discipline. I do not use the word "work" because anything to do with teaching riding and being with horses and the people who love them is "pleasure" to me.

The responsibility of caring for horses (the fact that they depend on you so completely) is always a rewarding experience. And teaching people to appreciate horses, teaching them to bring out the best in the animal as well as themselves, may seem to be a never-ending task but I find it an altogether enjoyable one.

Working with the horse in an understanding manner, caring for the horse so that he is content, and never abusing the animal, either through ignorance or ill temper, are points of responsibility the beginning rider should bear in mind. They're just as important as riding correctly—even more so.

VICTOR HUGO VIDAL, JR.
President, Cedar Lodge Farm
Stamford, Connecticut

INTRODUCTION

Riding is more popular today than at any time since the automobile nudged the horse off the nation's highways. The reasons are not hard to find.

Riding can be enjoyed by youngsters of both sexes and almost any age. Good size and notable strength are not essential qualities.

Riding can be enjoyed in virtually every part of the country at just about any time of the year. There is pleasure in riding by yourself, with your family, or with a group of friends.

One other benefit of riding is that it's a "lifetime sport." Learn when you're young and you're likely to enjoy it as long as you live. Football and baseball can't make that claim.

At what age can a youngster begin riding? The answer, of course, depends; it depends on the person's size, strength, and degree of physical coordination. Generally speaking, a boy or girl of nine or ten has the size and the strength to properly control and command a horse, although youngsters oftentimes begin riding at an even earlier age.

You will gain the greatest pleasure from riding if you learn slowly and correctly. This means you will have to have instruction, plus the use of a well-mannered horse. Both of these are available in riding academies. Look in the Yellow Pages of your telephone directory for riding academies in your area.

After ten to twelve hours of private instruction, you should be able to start, stop, and turn a horse.

You should also be able to post a trot and perhaps even sit a canter.

Styles of riding vary, but whether you learn "English-style" (sometimes called "Eastern") or "Western-style," really is not important, even though the two are different as to technique and the type of equipment used. English riding was developed in Great Britain by the wellborn and well-bred and brought to this country by the early Colonists. It was a style of riding suited for transportation and recreation—for fox hunts, steeplechases, and polo matches. Western riding, which can be traced back to the sixteenth-century Spanish conquerors in North America, had more practical uses. This style developed with the Western frontier and was used for such rugged ranch chores as cutting cattle and roping.

But riding transcends styles. It is a matter of horse handling and, English or Western, certain fundamentals apply. In your own case, simply follow the style that prevails in your area.

A final word: riding is much more than the business of mounting a horse, controlling him as he moves forward, to the right or left, as he trots, canters, and all the rest. That, really, is only the beginning. Riding is an art. And, to quote one expert horseman, ". . . as in every art, detail assumes a stature far beyond its apparent importance; a horse only goes well when accurately and quietly ridden." And it is from riding "accurately" and "quietly" that real enjoyment of the sport is derived.

CONTENTS

THE HORSE

The horse, by providing the joy of riding, is today regarded primarily as a source of pleasure. But such was not always the case. The animal has gone through several phases since being tamed and domesticated some four thousand years ago.

Scientists have established that horses were present on the North American continent in prehistoric times, but when Columbus landed in America, he found no horses. They had disappeared a few thousand years before, perhaps killed off by a fatal disease or by their inability to adapt to sharp changes in climate that had taken place.

The horse was reintroduced to North America during the fifteenth and sixteenth centuries. Columbus brought horses to the West Indies on his second voyage in 1493. Hernando Cortés used more than a thousand Spanish horses in his conquest of Mexico during the years from 1519 to 1521. The ships of Hernando de Soto, Francisco Vásquez de Coronado, and other Spanish explorers also carried horses to the New World. These animals became the foundation for the small, hardy horses of the American plains, called "mustangs." They were the horses used and prized by the Indians, who became expert riders.

In Colonial America, the horse was somewhat neglected at first. Oxen were the most important source of power until the eighteenth century when roads began to improve and light-legged mounts and draft horses, used for pulling loads, were imported.

Year by year, the horse took on increased importance in agriculture and transportation. A century ago the hitching post and watering trough were as common as the parking meter and gasoline pump are today. The horse population in the United States reached its peak in 1918, when the U. S. Department of Agriculture reported the total number to be 26,723,000.

But the age of the automobile was dawning, and with the automobile came the truck and a great array of other gasoline-engined machines. The need for horses dwindled steadily. By 1960, the year the Department of Agriculture discontinued counting horses, the number had fallen to a low of 3,089,000.

During the 1960's the horse staged a remarkable comeback, however. It is estimated that there are now more than seven million, and 85 per cent of these are saddle horses. Don Burt of Los Angeles, voted the best horse judge in the United States in 1968, has a reasonable explanation for the horse's new and growing popularity. "Our whole civilization is built upon the horse; it's part of our heritage," says Mr. Burt. "As we get more citified, there's more demand for release, for open spaces. Today, people can afford horses, so the sport is bound to grow."

Horses of prehistoric times were wild and ran free, roaming in large herds in search of grass and other vegetation. Since the horse was poorly equipped to defend himself, he learned to rely on speed to escape his enemies. In addition, he developed an extraordinary "early warning system."

His ears, though small in proportion to his size, are capable of detecting the faintest sounds. His sense of smell is so highly developed that he can scent far-off water or fresh grass. His eyes, large and bulbous, are set to the side of his face, enabling him to see objects not only ahead and to the side, but to the rear as well. The horse still has the impulse to run when one of his senses reports that danger threatens, a fact you should remember.

Of course, seldom will two horses react in precisely the same way to a given situation. There are, from a standpoint of temperament, a multiple of different types. As this suggests, a riding technique that is successful with one horse may not "work" with another, which is, incidentally, one of the fascinations of riding.

The appearance and condition of a horse's teeth indicate his age. The expression "long in the tooth" is, when speaking of horses, very meaningful. As the animal grows older, certain physical changes take place in the teeth that are recognizable by an expert. An experienced horseman can determine a

"Our whole civilization is built upon the horse; it's part of our heritage."

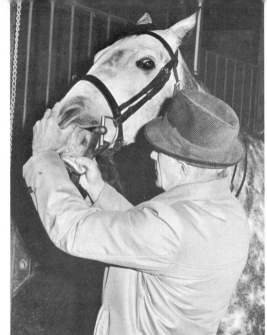

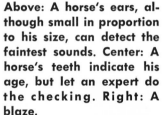

Above: A horse's ears, although small in proportion to his size, can detect the faintest sounds. Center: A horse's teeth indicate his age, but let an expert do the checking. Right: A blaze.

horse's age quite accurately up to about ten to fifteen years. After that it becomes increasingly difficult.

A horse reaches maturity at the age of seven, but many horses are very active at twice that age and beyond.

A filly is a female horse under the age of four. After a filly's fourth birthday, she is a mare. (All Thoroughbred horses are registered with birthdays of January 1, regardless of the actual date.) A colt is a male horse until the age of four. He then becomes a stallion, unless he has been castrated, in which case he is a gelding. Male riding horses are usually geldings.

The height of a horse is measured in units called "hands" A hand is equal to four inches, and the measurement is taken from the ground to the highest point of the withers, which is the highest point on the horse's back. A horse of about 15.2 hands is an average size, suitable for the average rider. Expert horsemen often prefer horses that range over sixteen hands.

When you describe a horse, be sure to use the proper term when speaking of his coloring. A bay horse is reddish brown, but the color can range from a reddish tan (called a light bay or sandy bay) to a deep mahogany (a dark or blood bay). A bay always has a black mane and tail and usually black lower legs.

A brown horse ranges from a rich, deep brown to almost black. Extremely dark bays and browns are frequently mistaken for blacks.

A chestnut horse can range from light shades (red and golden chestnut, or sorrel) to a deep copper, or dark chestnut. The mane and tail are about the same color or sometimes lighter than the body hairs, never black. Grays are a mixture of white and black hairs. All black at birth, they gradually lighten, sometimes turning completely white.

Roan is any solid color with a mixture of white hairs throughout. A strawberry roan is chestnut mixed with white. The red roan is a roaned bay color and the lower legs are usually black. Blue roans have reddish hairs mixed in with roaned black hairs.

Horses are also identified and described by the white markings they carry. A broad band of white extending down the front of a horse's face is called a blaze. A patch of white on the forehead is known as a star. A white mark at or between the horse's nostrils is called a snip. A white leg is termed a stocking.

One of the foremost principles of a noted horse trainer of the mid-nineteenth century was, "A good horseman should know neither fear nor anger." It is as meaningful today as it was a century ago.

All horses respond to gentleness and kindness. The best evidence of this is the Arabian horse, regarded by man as the most intelligent of all breeds. Experts say that the Arabian's superior ability to understand comes as a result of the affectionate treatment the breed received throughout the centuries. It was not uncommon for an Arab sheik to regard his favorite horse as if he were a member of the family, often having him share his tent. The Arabian horse learned to warn his master of approaching danger and performed feats of incredible heroism on the field of battle.

Left: A stocking.
Below: A star.

The stylish, long-legged Thoroughbred is supreme on the race courses of the world.

The Standardbred is the American trotting and pacing horse.

THE BREEDS

The horse you first ride will probably be the one most readily available. But even though you may not have much of a choice to begin with, it is well to be familiar with the various breeds of horses, and to appreciate the dominate characteristics of each.

Many people have confused ideas about breeds. Some of the confusion stems from the word "Thoroughbred" (with a capital T). More than a few people use the word when they actually mean *purebred*. To be precise, Thoroughbred is a breed of horse developed in England in the early 1700's by crossing Arabian stallions with English mares. All Thoroughbreds are registered, with a complete chart of breeding on record. In the United States, only properly registered Thoroughbreds are eligible for such famed races as the Kentucky Derby, the Preakness Stakes, and the Belmont Stakes.

Thoroughbreds are noted for their great speed and valiant spirit and are supreme on the race courses of the world. They cover ground with long, smooth strides, and are much sought after for both jumping and hunting.

The *hunter,* known for his speed as well as his jumping ability, is usually at least half Thoroughbred. Though spirited, the hunter is well-mannered, and he takes naturally to open country. The hunter is the strain of horse pictured in the instructional sequences of this book.

12

The term *Standardbred* refers to an American breed of trotting and pacing horse used primarily for harness racing. Occasionally a Standardbred will be used as a saddle horse, but because they have been taught to trot against the pull of a light carriage, they are more difficult to handle than the saddle-schooled animal.

The oldest of all horse strains is the *Arabian,* a gentle horse with exceptional intelligence and incredible stamina. It has been said that an Arabian can cover fifty to sixty miles in a single day, and keep it up day after day. The lineage of this breed can be traced far back into history, to a time before the birth of Christ.

The Arabian is regal in appearance, with an arched neck, flowing tail, alert eyes, and delicate, narrow ears. The disc-shaped bones of the cheek are

The proud Arabian is the oldest of all horse strains.

large and distinctive. He is graceful and lively, and his smooth gait makes him much-prized as a pleasure horse. Despite these noble qualities, the popularity of the Arabian in the United States has not been as notable as that of some other breeds. In Colonial times, the Arabian was too costly and too scarce to breed on a large scale. In addition, the Arabian is relatively small in size and, as a result was never trained in the West for roping, cutting, and other ranch tasks. And in both the West and East, big men felt a trifle absurd on the Arabian's back. Recently, however, the Arabian has come into vogue in many places. There were approximately 50,000 registered in the United States in 1969; there were less than 20,000 registered Arabians in 1959.

Neither the Thoroughbred, the Standardbred, or the Arabian suited the requirements of early Americans. There was a need for a horse with stamina for long treks, gaits that would give a comfortable ride, and style—beauty and refinement enough to impress one's friends and neighbors. You may recognize these as the characteristics of the American Saddle Horse, a sophisticated and ever-fashionable animal, well known for his snappy, high-stepping gaits.

The American Saddle Horse, sometimes called the "Saddler," may be either three-gaited or five-gaited. The gaits of the three-gaited animal are the walk, trot, and canter. The five-gaited Saddler, often

13

called the "Kentucky horse," performs these gaits: the walk, the slow gait (a sort of running walk), the trot, the canter, and the rack (an extremely fast but smooth gait, faster than the canter). But no matter how he is gaited, the Saddler provides a delightful ride.

The American Saddle Horse has a close relative in the Tennessee Walking Horse, a handsome, well-mannered, three-gaited animal that is named for his most noted gait, a spirited running walk. The versatile, easy-tempered Morgan, primarily an Eastern type until recent years, is still another all-American breed. Although relatively small, the Morgan is strong enough for work, yet fast enough for pleasure riding.

The nation's most popular breed is the Quarter Horse. (Thoroughbreds are a close second.) A cross-breed, the Quarter Horse first came to notice during the Colonial period as a race horse whose specialty was the dashing sprint. His name was derived from the distance he often raced so well, a quarter of a mile. As the popularity of racing increased, Thoroughbreds were imported, and the day of the Quarter Horse seemed to be at a close. Not at all; the breed went West. His quick starts, incredible maneuverability, and sure-footedness won the Quarter Horse a place as the faithful partner of the working cowhand.

But Quarter Horses are bred for many other purposes besides ranch tasks. They have been crossed

14

The American Saddle Horse is well known for his high-stepping gaits.

with Thoroughbreds to emphasize the quality of speed. Quarter Horse racing flourishes in many areas of the Southwest. Other Quarter Horses are bred to reinforce the original stocky, heavy-muscled appearance of the breed.

While the Quarter Horse may be the most popular of breeds, particularly in the West, it is the Appaloosa that is usually designated as the original Western horse. The first frontiersmen to push westward found large herds of these horses in the hands of the Indians, and the type was particularly favored among the Indians of the Palouse River country in the southwest corner of what is now the state of Washington.

The Appaloosa's most distinctive characteristic is, of course, his unusual spotting, which takes the

The Appaloosa is known for its distinctive spotting.

The rugged Quarter Horse is the country's most popular breed.

form of small, dark circular splotches that appear against a light background. Usually they pattern the horse's hindquarters and rump. Frequently he has vertically striped hoofs, too. The Appaloosa is a sensible, sure-footed animal, with gaits that are easy and comfortable.

Westerners also have a fancy for two other color strains, the palomino and the pinto. The palomino is usually of Quarter Horse stock and is characterized by his golden color and flaxen mane and tail.

15

The pinto, also known as the paint horse, features large blotches of white against a coat of color, or dark tones against a light background. Whatever the specifics, the pinto is invariably a flashy mount.

While strains of horses tend to develop along regional lines, there are palominos and Appaloosas in the East, and Saddlers in the West. The trend is toward the spread of all breeds to all sections.

As you have probably judged, the strains of horses meant for saddle use have reached an advanced state of development in the United States. The horse you ride is likely to represent well over a century of specialized environment, selective breeding, and careful training.

TACK

Tack is the gear used in equipping a horse, including the saddle, bridle, and bit. As a beginning rider, your horse will undoubtedly be "tacked up" and led out for you each day you ride. But even so, it is well to know all you can about the various pieces of equipment so that you can use it intelligently.

The *bridle* is the head harness which, in combination with the *reins,* is used to guide the horse. A main feature of the bridle is a metal mouthpiece called the *bit.* On each side of the horse's mouth there is a gap between his incisors—his front teeth —and molars. The bit fits through these two gaps and rests on the horse's tongue.

There are several types of bits, but the young rider usually uses a *snaffle bit*, which consists of a joined bar with a large metal ring at each end. The reins are attached to the rings. A snaffle bridle of course, is one that employs a snaffle bit.

The reins, working through the bit, afford a means of communicating with the horse. A horse's mouth is sensitive and he can feel even the slightest pressure of the bit, applied through use of the reins. A well-trained horse will react to the mere intent to apply pressure; that is, to the lifting of the reins. The bit should never be regarded as a means of coercion. Neither should the bridle or reins be considered as an aid to the rider's balance.

17

Another type of bridle and bit is the *Pelham.* It requires a second set of reins called *curb reins.* When pulled, the curb reins act to apply pressure underneath the horse's chin by means of a *curb chain* as well as inside the horse's mouth. Only an experienced rider should use a Pelham.

The English saddle, the type generally used at riding academies, is constructed of several layers of leather upon a light wooden frame called a *tree.* It is held in place on the horse's back by means of a belt known as a *girth.*

The girth is buckled to straps on the saddle that are called *billets.* A leather flap beneath protects the horse from being scratched by the buckles. An outer flap, sometimes called a *skirt,* protects the horse

Below right: the standing martingale (left) and the running martingale

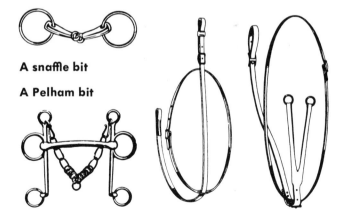

A snaffle bit

A Pelham bit

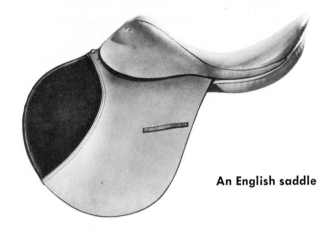

An English saddle

from these buckles and also protects the rider from the horse's sweat.

The *stirrups* hang down outside the skirt. The rider's feet go into the *stirrup irons*. Buckles on the stirrup straps allow each to be shortened or lengthened.

The front part of the saddle is known as the *pommel*; the hind part, which usually curves upward, is called the *cantle*. The English saddle has a relatively low cantle and pommel, full side flaps that are usually set forward, and a well-padded leather seat. The Western saddle is heavier; it has a deep seat and high pommel, a pommel horn, and wide leather flaps to protect the rider's legs. It also has little seat padding. In general, English equipment is lighter and more flexible. It is easier on the horse and rider. The English saddle is excellent for train-

ing, and preferred for hunting and jumping.

The *martingale* is a piece of restraining harness that some horses wear. Its purpose is to steady or hold down the horse's head. The *standing martingale* consists of a strap that fastens to the girth, passes between the forelegs, through a loop in the neck strap, and is attached to the noseband. The *running martingale* also fastens to the girth, passes between the forelegs and through the neck strap, but it divides at the chest into two branches, each of which ends in a ring through which the reins pass. It is regarded by many to be more efficient than the standing martingale.

The *breastplate* is a part of the harness that runs across the horse's chest and is used—mostly on slender horses—to keep the saddle from slipping to the rear.

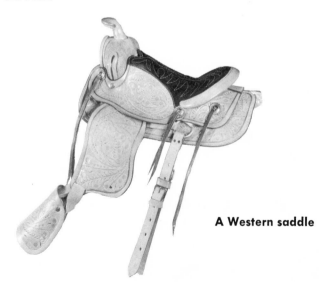

A Western saddle

WHAT TO WEAR

If you are serious about riding, you should groom yourself properly for the sport. There's no rule of etiquette that says you cannot wear old clothes for a riding lesson in the country, but you'll be more comfortable and ride better if you are properly outfitted.

The correct riding outfit consists of breeches (or jodhpurs), boots, and a riding coat. Both breeches and jodhpurs are trousers that are cut full over the hips, and taper in at the knee. Breeches end below the calf; jodhpurs are tight fitting from the knee to the ankle. The styles of breeches and jodhpurs vary from place to place, depending on the type of horse and saddle common to the area. Whether you choose breeches or jodhpurs, they should fit the knee snugly. Otherwise, they are likely to cause chafing, since you use your knees to control the horse.

Be certain your breeches button well down the leg so they won't work up and wrinkle at the knee. Stretch breeches have helped to eliminate the problem of wrinkly knees, but they are more expensive than conventional gabardine.

Take particular care in selecting your boots. Be sure they are the right length. When new, they should be high enough to just touch the back tendon at the hollow of the knee. They should fit the leg snugly. Boots that are loose about the calf look poorly and are no help to you as a rider.

19

The proper riding outfit consists of a protective riding cap, hip length jacket, breeches, and boots.

This young rider wears an attractive vest-shirt combination beneath her jacket.

Boots, when new, should be high enough in the back to just touch the leg tendons.

Take care of your boots by cleaning them as soon after use as possible. Use castile or glycerin soap on a sponge that has been dipped in lukewarm water and well-squeezed. After the boots have been left standing for an hour, apply a light coat of leather conditioner. To polish them, use a boot cream, not a paste. Apply sparingly.

Never attempt to dry out the boots in the sun or near a radiator. When storing, use boot trees to prevent wrinkles at the ankle; boot-legger trees will keep the legs of the boots in proper shape. .

For your personal safety, and to make a nice appearance as well, you may want to equip yourself with a protective riding cap, the type that features a hard outer shell with either cushioned inner padding or an adjustable headband. Most styles are covered in black velvet.

A riding jacket is not essential for the beginner. Any neat, hip-length jacket will do. Gloves—leather or string—should be worn, both summer and winter. They help to guard against blisters and will not slip on the reins.

If you do not wear a conventional riding outfit, whatever you do wear should be of a subdued nature. Bluejeans are often acceptable, but a boy should never wear a "loud" sports shirt, nor a girl a garish blouse. Loafers or sneakers are not a wise choice because you will not have proper or safe footing in the stirrups. Sturdy shoes with a slight heel are next best to boots.

LEADING A HORSE

A horse is a sensitive animal. If frightened he may kick or jump. This nervous reaction is part of the horse's heritage, and traces back to the time when the animal ran wild and anything that moved was likely to be an enemy. This does not mean that you should be afraid of horses. Simply be careful whenever you are about them.

It does not mean that you should choose a lazy or spiritless mount when you are learning to ride. Of course, you will want a quiet and well-behaved horse, but he should be alert and have a willing disposition.

Never make a sudden or abrupt movement when near a horse. Never come up to one unexpectedly. Whenever you approach a horse, speak to him. Be sure he knows you are there, Repeat his name; pat him gently on the nose or neck.

Even the best mannered of horses may kick nervously if he senses anything in back of him. Keep a sharp eye on the horse's heels if you must go behind him.

To lead a horse, walk up alongside his left shoulder. (A horse is always handled from the left side. He has been trained that way. If you approach from the right, you may startle him.)

Grasp the reins in your right hand about six inches beneath the bit. The ends of the reins should be looped over the horse's withers, the highest part

21

of his back, or you can hold the ends in your left hand. This is the best practice to follow if you are not going to mount him right away. In any case, don't let the ends drag on the ground. You or the horse could trip over them.

Once you have taken hold of the reins, face in the same direction as the horse and walk forward slowly. The horse will walk beside you. No horse will intentionally step on your feet, but if you put your foot in his path he may not see it.

When you approach a horse, speak to him. Pat him gently on the nose or neck.

Suppose the horse does not want to move. He plants his feet firmly and balks. The thing to do is to grasp the reins as described above, and turn his head sharply, first to the right and then to the left. He will have to step to the side to keep his balance, and once he begins to move it is likely he will keep going.

To back a horse, stand to the left of his head and face him. Grasp the reins in your left hand about six inches from the bit. Pull firmly toward the rear. At the same time, put your right hand on his shoul-

Left: When leading a horse, walk alongside his left shoulder.

Below: To back a horse, stand to the left of his head and face him. Pull with the left hand . . .

... **while pressing with the right.**

der point and press firmly. He will step slowly backward.

Don't attempt to ride until you are perfectly at ease with your horse. Being confident in his presence is just as important as knowing how to mount, sit, and use the reins.

HOW TO MOUNT

Always mount from the horse's left side, his "near" side. This is what the horse expects. (The right side is called the "off" side.)

If the horse has been led out for you, first check the tack. Is the girth secure? Are the stirrups of the right length? Is the bit placed properly in the horse's mouth? Is the saddle on correctly? Of course, if you've tacked up the horse yourself, this should not be necessary.

Face slightly toward the rear (your own left shoulder beside the horse's left shoulder). At the same time, collect the reins in your left hand over the horse's withers, holding them tight enough to gain control of the horse, but loose enough so that you can grasp the horse's mane to help pull yourself up. Let the ends of the reins drop to the right of the horse's neck.

With your right hand, turn the stirrup and adjust the stirrup iron on your left foot. Then grasp the cantle, the rear part of the saddle, with your right hand.

Now it's simply a matter of pushing off with your right foot while pulling your body upward with both arms. Balancing on the left stirrup, swing your right leg over the horse's rump, and gently lower your weight into the saddle. The important word is "gently"; never drop into the saddle abruptly. Once seated, ease your right foot into the right stirrup.

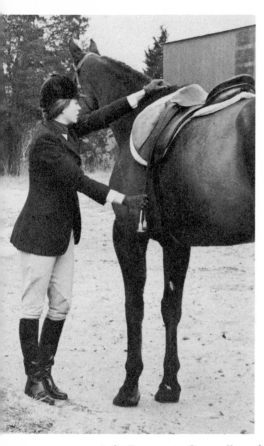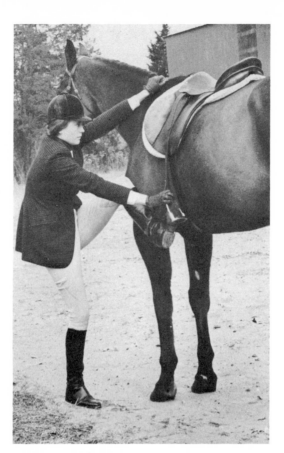

Left: To mount, first collect the reins in your left hand; then grasp the horse's mane. Center: Adjust the stirrup iron on your left foot. Right: Grasp the cantle with your right hand; push off with your right foot.

When you are confronted by a horse that moves his hindquarters away from you as you start to mount, shorten the outside rein, the right rein, and turn the horse's head away from you. If he then takes a step, his hindquarters will move toward you and you will be able to mount.

A word of caution: in preparing to mount, be careful to insert your boot in the stirrup iron only up to the ball of the foot. Otherwise, your boot toe is liable to jab the horse in the ribs as your body turns, which will startle him.

You show your skill in mounting by being smooth and graceful. There should be no abrupt movements, or scrambling.

Swing your right leg over the horse's rump.

Be careful to insert your boot only up to the ball of the foot.

When adjusting a stirrup, maintain a slight downward pressure on the stirrup iron. Let the strap slide slowly through your fingers until the leather is of proper length.

To adjust the girth, first swing your left foot forward, then take up the girth by a notch or two.

ADJUSTING THE STIRRUPS AND GIRTH

Your stirrups must hang evenly and be of the right length. When you are beginning to ride, your instructor will advise you as to the proper length. One rule of thumb says that when you remove your feet from the stirrups, the bottom of the stirrup iron should be even with the point of your ankle bone.

To adjust a stirrup, grasp the reins in one hand. Keep your foot in the stirrup iron and maintain slight downward pressure. Grasp the end of the stirrup leather near the buckle and pull up to open the buckle. Continue to press downward on the iron. Let the strap slide slowly through your fingers until the leather is of proper length. Then rebuckle.

Don't look down when making this adjustment. Do it by "feel." By keeping your body erect, you remain in a "ready" position, which is vital should the horse start forward.

Once mounted, you may find the girth is not quite tight enough. Some horses swell themselves up when being saddled. After the rider has been in the saddle for a short time, the animal relaxes and his dimensions reduce to normal. This eccentricity should cause you no problem. With your foot in the stirrup, swing your left foot forward of the girth. Hold the reins in your right hand, pull up the flap and take up the girth by a notch or two.

Bear in mind that most girths have three billet straps. Don't buckle any one of them tighter than the others.

HOW TO DISMOUNT

Dismounting, like mounting, should be from the horse's left side.

Collect the reins in your left hand, holding them short enough to maintain control. Also with your left hand, grasp the horse's mane or neck. Remove your right foot from its stirrup, and swing your right leg back over the horse's rump, at the same time grasping the cantle or the saddle's far edge with your right hand.

Balance for a moment in the left stirrup; both knees should be straight. Now lean your weight over the saddle and remove your left foot from its stirrup. Then, pushing away from the saddle, simply slide to the ground, landing squarely on both feet.

What you must *not* attempt to do is lower yourself to the ground one leg at a time. This method, which implies that the left foot will remain in the stirrup until the right foot touches down, can prove dangerous should the horse decide to move forward.

In dismounting, swing your right leg back over the horse's rump.

28

Balance for a moment in the left stirrup, then lean your weight on the saddle and remove your left foot from the stirrup.

Last, pushing yourself away from the saddle, slide to the ground.

Rockwood Area Elementary
School Library

ACCESSION NO. 3169

POSITION IN THE SADDLE

Position is a matter of getting a "good seat." It is as essential to your success in the sport as control of the reins and a well-fitting saddle, and is a subject that will concern you for as long as you ride.

Correct position is important not only because it "feels right" and gives a stylish appearance but, more important, it allows you maximum use of the "aids"—your legs and hands, the reins, and your weight—in controlling the horse.

The right position is attained largely by balance,

When your position is right, your head is up and your shoulders square. Your back should be erect but not stiff.

not strength. When you mount, plant your weight in the center of the saddle, but do not lean on your buttocks or rest back on the base of your spine. Instead, support yourself on your thighs. Your weight should be balanced over the stirrups. In other words, do not sit on the horse as you do on a chair. It's almost as though you were standing upright, with the inside of your thighs gripping the horse's back.

Press your upper calf and knees to the saddle. At the same time, flex your ankles inward so that you force your feet and lower legs away from the horse's sides. Your heels should be lower than your toes, with the toes pointing outward slightly.

Many expert riders advise the rider to keep the foot to the inside of the stirrup tread. This tends to force the knees into proper contact with the saddle flap.

Keep your head up and your shoulders square. Your back should be erect, but not stiff.

Your elbows should be close to your sides. Your hands, holding the reins a few inches apart, should be just above and in front of the horse's withers.

It takes time and plenty of conscious effort to learn the correct position. But it is time well spent, for the highest jumps and fastest gaits rely upon these essentials, with only slight modifications.

Be sure to have an instructor check and recheck you at this stage. Working in an indoor ring that is equipped with a mirror is an excellent way to help you learn proper position.

Press your upper calf and knees to the saddle. Your heels should be lower than your toes, with the toes pointing outward slightly.

USING YOUR HANDS

To control your horse, you rely upon the "aids" —your legs and hands, the reins, and the weight of your body. Every maneuver is accomplished by means of one aid or a combination of them.

As a beginning rider, you should concentrate on using your hands correctly. The idea is to handle the horse smoothly, without much pull on the reins, and to control him should he become excited, without much pressure on the bit. When you are able to do this, you will be said to have "good hands."

When grasping the reins, keep your knuckles vertical, your thumbs on top.

Some riders grasp each rein in a fist. Others prefer to use a three-finger grip, with the rein coming between the fourth and the little finger. Either way, the reins should be held firmly but not stiffly.

These instructions refer to a snaffle bridle; that is, to one set of reins. But if you are using a Pelham, you will have two sets of reins to contend with. The grip is much the same, however. The curb rein should be on the bottom, the snaffle on top. To keep the two apart, place your fourth and little finger in between them. The curb rein should be held more loosely than the snaffle.

Some riders prefer this three-finger grip.

Your arm from the elbow should form a straight line with the rein to the horse's mouth.

As a beginning rider, your hands should be "quiet." That is, they should maintain only the lightest pressure. With each ride, increase the pressure slightly until you reach a stage where the reins are, as one expert describes it, "softly taut."

Keep your forearms parallel to the horse. Your knuckles should be vertical, your thumbs on top. Your arms, from the elbow, should form a straight line with the reins to the horse's mouth.

One cannot stress too much the importance of keeping your hands quiet and still. Never move them needlessly. Never "wave" your elbows and arms.

Never use the reins to support your weight or in an attempt to keep your balance. Doing any one of these things will cause you to signal the horse, but it will be a false signal. The horse can become confused, excited, and probably disobedient.

It must be said that no two horses react to the hands on the reins in exactly the same way. A stable horse with "some years on him," one that is used to having people pull and tug at his mouth, is likely to require relatively sharp signals. A sensitive, spirited mount will respond to the slightest pull. Thus, it is important to get the "feel" of the horse right away.

33

TURNING

You can practice turning astride your horse while in place. Be sure to maintain even pressure on the reins.

When you want to turn the horse left, increase the tension on the left rein, and simultaneously relax the pressure on the right rein. Close your left calf against the horse's side.

To turn the horse right, simply do the opposite—increase the tension on the right rein, and at the same time relax the pressure on the left rein. Close your right calf against the horse's side.

English-style riders always ride with both hands

Practice turning while astride your horse, but in place. Keep even pressure on the reins.

on the reins. But those who ride Western style hold the reins in one hand. (Traditionally, the cowboy must have his right hand free for roping and other work.)

To ride as a Western rider, grip both reins in your left hand, with the hand over the horse's withers. The thumb is on top, the knuckles vertical.

To turn left, twist your left hand toward the left and increase the tension in the left rein. Practice astride the horse, while in place. Close your left calf to the horse's body.

To turn right, bend your arm at the wrist so as to impart tension on the right rein. Close your right calf to the horse's body.

To turn left, increase the pressure on the left rein. At the same time, close your left calf to the horse's side.

USING YOUR LEGS

The legs operate in combination with the other aids in controlling and guiding the horse.

Recall how your legs are positioned as you sit astride the horse. You are gripping the horse with your upper thighs while your knees are "hugging" the saddle flap.

Your legs can be used to control the horse's hindquarters. Keep in mind that the horse's inclination is to move his hindquarters *away* from the leg pressure. If you wish the horse to swing his hindquarters to the left, apply pressure with the right calf. Keep the knee tight to the saddle flap. Also press your right heel at a point about six inches behind the girth. If you wish the horse to swing his hindquarters to the right, apply pressure with the left calf and heel.

Your weight is another very helpful aid. When you lean forward, you change the distribution of your weight, and the horse will move forward to restore the balance.

When you lean back, the horse has an inclination to bring his legs under him to bring your weight into even balance. In other words, he steps back.

Your legs control the horse's hindquarters. If you wish the horse to swing right . . .

. . . simply apply pressure
with your left calf.

STARTING AND STOPPING

If you are able to mount and take the correct position on the horse, and understand how to hold your hands and change direction while astride the horse in place, you should have no trouble controlling a horse in motion—walking.

Once mounted, settle yourself in the saddle. Grip the horse with your thighs; press your knees firmly against the saddle flap.

Maintain slight pressure on the reins. When you want the horse to move forward, use your heels to apply slight pressure to the horse just behind the girth. Your knees should remain in position; only the lower leg and heel swing free. You don't have to jab the horse with your heels. A slight squeeze is all that is necessary.

At the same time that you apply pressure with your heels, lean forward slightly.

As the horse moves ahead, maintain your proper position in the saddle. Keep your head erect. Avoid looking down to the ground; look between the horse's ears to see where you are going and if there is anything in the path—a rock, a log, a hole. Hold your hands steady. Keep your elbows close to your sides.

Relax! Get accustomed to the "feel" of the horse. Walk him about; turn him.

To stop, increase the pressure on both reins simultaneously. A stiff yank is not necessary. A steady, gentle pull is what to strive for. The horse should not be jerked to a sudden stop.

When you want to move forward, use your heels to apply pressure behind the girth.

38

As the horse moves, maintain your proper position in the saddle. Keep your head erect, shoulders square.

To stop, increase the tension on both reins simultaneously.

THE TROT

After you have learned to take the proper position on the horse, and to control him at a walk, you are ready for the next phase—the trot.

The walk and trot are two of the horse's gaits. Two others are the canter and the gallop.

The trot is a two-beat gait. The horse's legs strike the ground in pairs—left rear and right foreleg, then right rear and left foreleg. Whenever a pair of legs moves forward, you are pushed upward and forward. Indeed, there is a substantial amount of up-and-down movement, and if you are not prepared for it, it can be hard to take. Yet the trot can be enjoyable to ride—if you post; that is, if you rise and descend from the saddle in harmony with the rhythm of the horse. It is not difficult to do.

To send the horse into a trot, press your heels firmly against the horse's side. To post, you rise in the stirrups and lean forward slightly, lifting your seat well out of the saddle. You stay at the peak of the post only long enough to miss a stride, then sit again. If you do it properly and with the correct tempo, you won't feel the slightest jostling.

Don't stand up abruptly and then fall back. In fact, when posting, you don't really stand in the stirrups but merely rest your weight on them and raise yourself out of the saddle. When an expert rider posts, you can hardly perceive that he is moving up and down. It looks effortless.

To post, rise in the stirrups and lean forward slightly.

As you post, maintain your knees in firm contact with the saddle flap. Your knee grip should be firm enough to control the fall of your body. All impact should be taken in the knee and ankle, not the seat.

Keep even pressure on the reins, but let your hands move with the action of the horse's head. Do not balance by the reins. Your elbows should always be at your sides.

Some instructors tell their pupils to sit in the

40

saddle as the horse trots and "take it" for a short period to learn the rhythmic pattern of the trot. This method also helps the young rider to learn to rise by getting an assist from the "up" action of the horse.

A good many horses have a gait between the walk and the trot, called a jog. Frequently it is so smooth that it can be ridden sitting down in the saddle as for a walk; that is, no posting is necessary. Riding a good jog is an excellent introduction to the trot. It enables you to become accustomed to the rhythm of the trot while developing your balance.

When you become skilled in posting, you should take notice of which *diagonal* you are posting on.

Do you rise when the right foreleg and left rear leg move forward, or when the left foreleg and right rear leg do? You can tell by glancing down at the horse's shoulder to see which of his forelegs is stretching forward. If you are riding a trot over a long distance, you should change diagonals occasionally so as not to tire the horse. To change, simply sit out one stride when you would ordinarily rise.

You will get more than a few rude bumps before you become accomplished at posting. Don't give up. It is simply a matter of learning the rhythm and moving your body accordingly. You should be able to acquire the skill in one or two practice sessions.

Stay up long enough to miss the stride, then sit again. When a horse trots, the strides are taken by diagonal

pairs of legs. Right: the left foreleg and right rear leg are reaching forward.

THE CANTER

The canter is a slow, controlled gallop. It is a three-beat, rocking-chair gait. With some horses, the canter is so smooth that the rider can sit comfortably in the saddle, although a beginner may find himself bouncing a good bit.

Most horses canter from a trot, but some will go into a canter directly from a walk. When you want your mount to canter, press one heel firmly against the horse's side and exert increased pressure on the rein on that side. Relax the pressure on the rein as soon as the horse begins to canter.

You should be firmly planted in the saddle. Some prefer to lean forward slightly, but be sure to keep your weight balanced over the stirrups. Maintain a firm grip with your inner thighs and knees. Keep your heels down, away from the animal, and your head erect. Don't stand up in the stirrups. Don't bend forward, jockey-style.

In the trot the matter of diagonals is very important, and in the canter you must be aware of *leads*. When a horse canters, one foreleg reaches farther out to the front than the other. If the leading

In the canter, remain firmly planted in the saddle. Keep your heels down, your head erect.

leg happens to be the horse's right foreleg, the animal is said to be on a right lead.

On a circular track or on any curve, the horse's inside leg should lead. For example, if the horse is circling to the right, he should be on a right lead—his right leg should be striking out farther than his left; otherwise, the mount will not be in proper balance and he will feel and look awkward.

Some horses—polo ponies, for instance—change leads automatically as they change direction. But the rider should always signal the horse to take the proper lead. If you want to put the horse into a right lead, press your left foot firmly against the horse's side and increase the pressure on the left rein. If you want the horse to move into a left lead, do the opposite—press with the right heel and increase the tension of the right rein.

When you are ready to trot or canter, your instructor may advise you to use a crop (also called a whip or a bat). The crop is an aid—like your hands or legs—to urge the horse ahead. Carry the crop in your right hand along with the rein. When you need to use the crop, switch the rein to your left hand. Strike the horse behind the girth.

This horse is on a left lead.

THE GALLOP

At the canter, most horses move at ten to twelve miles an hour; at an extended gallop, a horse's speed is almost twice that. Obviously, this calls for some changes in the rider's "seat." As one expert declares, you should "float close to the saddle (at the gallop), rather than sit in it."

To move the horse into a gallop from a canter, simply apply pressure with your calves. Once the horse moves out, relax the pressure, but be alert to apply it again should he not maintain proper speed.

Lean forward from the waist, but keep your back straight. Shorten the reins. Your thighs and knees should maintain contact with the saddle, but raise your buttocks.

Never try to stop the horse abruptly. Stopping is a slowing down process. Apply even pressure on the reins. When the horse responds by slowing, ease the pressure. Then apply it again. Wait for the response, then release. The horse is likely to go from a gallop, to a canter, to a trot, to a walk, and then halt.

If the horse feels as though he may be getting out of hand, apply even pressure on the reins, releasing it as soon as he responds. This will usually serve to restrain him.

When the horse moves into a gallop, lean forward from the waist. Keep your back straight. Shorten the reins.

The matter of leads is important. As noted earlier, when riding on a circular course, the horse's inside leg should lead.

Anytime you are moving at a rapid gait, keep particularly alert. A wise rider learns to anticipate his horse's reactions. As a rule, horses are easily shaken. A dog coming at your mount unexpectedly, a blowing bit of paper, or reflected light from a window pane or any piece of glass may upset even a well-behaved horse. An abrupt shy at fast pace can be dangerous.

Only a few surfaces are really suitable for so fast a pace as a gallop. There must be good cushioning or the horse is likely to develop one or more leg ailments. As the pace increases so does the strain on his legs. Turf is best for the gallop.

JUMPING

Horses are natural jumpers. They will leap surprising heights and distances in quest of better grazing area, to join horses in another field, or in time of danger. In taking a horse over a jump, it is a matter of positioning your body in such a way that you do not limit the horse's freedom of action, his natural aptitude to take the jump.

If you are planning to try jumping, you should be skilled at the trot, canter, and gallop. Indeed, you must be able to ride almost as if you are part of the horse. While experience is vital, so also is confidence.

You must have a poised and assured attitude toward jumping. Horses are quick to sense the slightest hesitancy on the part of the rider. Once this happens, calamity is likely to result.

As a beginner, your mount should be an experienced and willing jumper. This does not mean that the horse has to be capable of jumping great heights, but he must be altogether agreeable about scaling low fences. You should never have any apprehension about your horse's performance. Your sole concern should be your technique. Naturally, the first fences you attempt should be low ones—a foot to a foot and a half in height.

The rider should remain well down in the saddle as he approaches, but he must lean forward slightly.

By rising and leaning forward, the rider gives the horse sufficient freedom of action to propel himself **over the barrier. Right: Perfect balance in the air.**

The key to a smart jump is a good approach. Some horses jump well from almost a standstill, while others need speed and go into a jump from a canter. You must know your mount.

As you near the jump, lift your weight from the saddle and lean forward. It is not just a simple bend from the waist; your buttocks must come completely out of the saddle. Your knees and legs will support your weight in the stirrups. Your hands move up

the horse's crest, or mane, to take the weight of your upper body. When a horse takes a jump, he is propelled over by his hindquarters. When you lift yourself and move your weight forward, you are giving him greater freedom to use his hindquarters.

When a horse jumps he extends his neck and lowers his head. Let your arms extend with him and give him plenty of rein. Once he is off the ground, the best thing a rider can do is not to interfere with him. Don't attempt to spring ahead or "jump" forward yourself as the horse goes over. Simply hold your balanced position.

Once over, sink slowly into the saddle, taking up the position for a canter. Keep the horse on a straight course for at least twenty feet.

This is elementary jumping. As you proceed to more advanced stages, there will be greater emphasis on bringing the horse to the jump with the proper amount of pace and balance, and releasing him for the jump at precisely the right instant. If your mount is too close to the jump when you release him, he will have to double up his body and "climb" over in awkward fashion. If your take-off point is too far back, the arc of the leap will be so wide it will be virtually impossible for you to get up and out of the saddle; you'll be "caught back." In addition, the *experienced rider* waits for the horse, when leaping up, to thrust him up and forward.

A horse may refuse a jump. This can be upsetting to a beginner and even cause a fall. But never stop jumping after a refusal. It may be necessary to lower the jump, but don't let the horse get into a habit of disobedience.

When the barrier is cleared the rider eases gently into the saddle.

After the jump, keep the horse on a straight course for at least twenty feet.

A perfectly timed jump, with the horse "released" at precisely the right instant.

TRAIL RIDING

It can vary from the well-worn bridle path of a city park to the narrow dirt roadway of an unspoiled forest tract, but trail riding is always one of the most glorious pleasures the sport of riding has to offer. Yet unless you are considerate of your mount and fellow riders, you will sharply limit both your enjoyment and satisfaction.

To preserve your mount, begin slowly. Walk for the first mile.

In a group, your pace should be that of the slowest horse. Never move your horse into a canter or a gallop if there is another horse beside you or if you are in a group. The other horse or horses will be inclined to break into a faster gait, too, and this can be hazardous if there are inexperienced riders along.

Ride in pairs whenever the trail is wide enough. The better rider should keep to the outside so that he is closest to any oncoming horses. When overtaking a group of riders, adjust the gait of your mount to that of the horses ahead, and then call out to the riders for permission to pass.

Never stay at the same gait for too long a period. Never allow your horse to overheat. If his flanks begin to heave or his breathing becomes labored, dismount and lead him.

Keep your weight well forward when negotiating uphill terrain. By doing this you take your weight off the horse's loins and place it on his shoulders. Centered there, it is easier to carry.

Investigate any lameness immediately. Sometimes this is caused by a stone that becomes wedged between the shoe and the inner and sensitive portion of the horse's foot. Simply dislodge the stone. If a shoe comes off, walk the horse back to the stable, being careful not to injure the unprotected foot.

In trail riding, never allow a horse to eat grass or leaves. Trail-sides nowadays are often sprayed with insecticides and herbicides, and either of these can do the animal serious harm, or even kill him. In addition, nibbling is a bad habit and can quickly lead to other disciplinary problems. If you cross a brook, allow the horse to drink if he wants to. But then

Before you set out, check the bridle to see that the harness is not twisted.

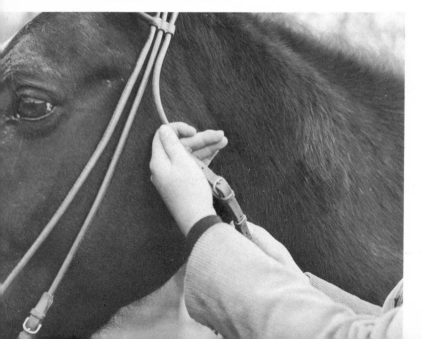

Ride in pairs whenever the
trail is wide enough.

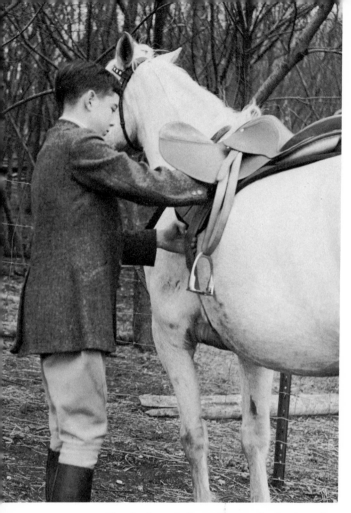

Check the girth at intervals during the ride.

If your horse goes lame, investigate right away.

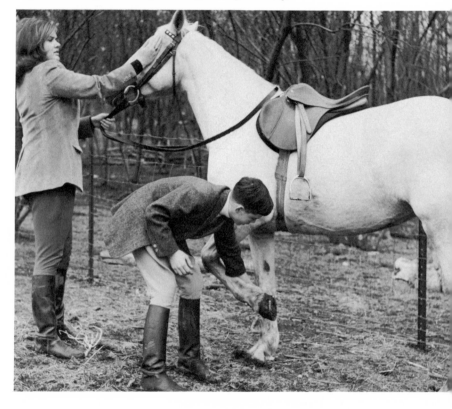

continue your ride; don't allow the horse to stand. Otherwise, he might be stricken with an attack of painful colic.

Check your tack periodically. Is the girth too tight? Is the horse developing saddle sores? Is the curb chain twisted?

Whenever a group approaches a sharp downhill grade or rough terrain, the leader should shorten his horse's stride to less than a full walk, and he should not increase the gait until the last rider has negotiated the troublesome stretch. Doing otherwise can cause horses in the rear to step up their pace at the wrong moment.

If your horse balks at passing some object, such as an odd-shaped rock formation, allow another horse and rider to go first. Press your calves to the horse's sides to urge him ahead. If the horse still refuses, have a mounted rider lead your horse by the cheek strap.

If your horse rears, don't panic. Shift your weight forward as far as you can. Don't tug on the reins. As he goes down, pull his head down with one rein and kick him with the opposite heel. You will force him to turn in a small circle and he cannot possibly rear. Then, get him moving. A horse can only rear from a standing-still position.

It is often said that a rider is not really experienced until he has been thrown from his mount at least three times. It happens to the best of riders but, surprisingly, even the most disastrous-looking spills

A hoof pick

usually are not serious to either horse or rider. The trick is to know how to fall. Let your body go limp and land like a rag doll. The horse will immediately scramble to its feet. Catch hold of the reins and walk him to be sure he is uninjured. Then remount right away if you hope to ride him successfully again.

Never chase a runaway horse, and don't try to head him off. The party should halt. When the runaway sees the other horses stop, he sometimes stops himself. If so, approach the horse on foot, talking quietly to him.

If you plan a day-long ride, schedule a two-hour rest period at midday. Loosen the saddle girth. Remove the bridle and tie the horse with a halter to a low-hanging tree limb. Keep the rope short. Otherwise, the horse may entangle himself.

It is common practice to walk the last mile. This serves to cool the horse gradually. If your horse is hot, dismount, loosen the girth, and lead him in.

YOUR OWN HORSE

Once you've become an accomplished rider—not necessarily an expert—you may begin to think about buying a horse of your own, and either boarding him at a nearby stable, or keeping him at home, providing, of course, you have an acre or two of grazing land.

According to the dictionary, the term "horse trader" means "a person who is shrewd and clever in bargaining." As this implies, buying a sound horse is not as easy as purchasing a bicycle, or even a new car. It takes superior knowledge and enormous experience. Get all the advice you can.

One person you should be sure to consult is a veterinarian who specializes in the treatment of horses. For a modest fee, he will examine the horse you are considering carefully, and advise you if the animal is plagued with any ailment or ailments that might impair his value.

Before you make the purchase, be sure to try the horse out under a variety of situations. Have other riders try him and get their opinions.

The horse you select should be well-suited to your skills. If you are well-trained and experienced, you don't want an "Old Nellie," a lifeless, plodding mount. On the other hand, if your experience is

Grooming starts with the curry comb. Note the use of a crosstie to keep the horse still.

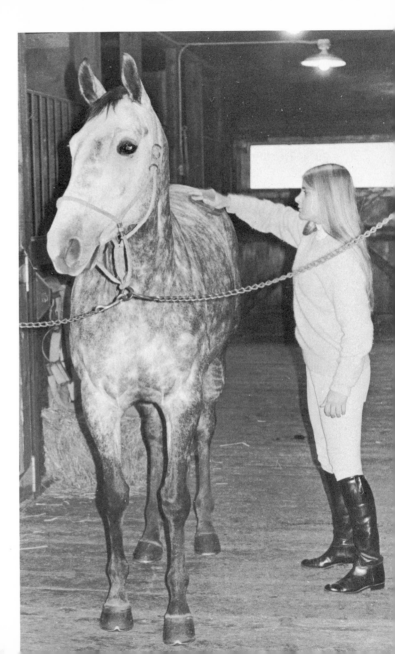

limited, be careful not to buy "too much" horse.

How much should you pay? It's difficult to make a general statement as to price, but from $500 to $1,000 there is a great array of worthwhile stock available. Your smartest investment is a healthy horse. Bear in mind that it costs as much to feed an inferior horse as it does a champion, and it often involves a great deal more trouble and expense to keep him in operating form.

Once you've purchased a horse, set a daily schedule for chores you must perform. These include feeding, grooming, and cleaning the horse's stall.

The horse did not get the sneering nickname "hay burner" by accident. Hay is a staple in every horse's diet. Not all hay is good hay, however. It should consist largely of timothy and clover, and be bright in color and sweet in smell. You should learn to recognize good hay from bad, but you really don't have to be an expert on the subject, for your horse, either by ignoring it or consuming it avidly, will make the evaluation. An active horse requires about thirty pounds of hay a day.

A horse also needs plenty of oats, the amount depending on how often he is ridden. It can be as much as twelve to fourteen quarts each day. The more he is worked, the more he needs. Oats provide energy and if you skimp on them you are likely to find your mount becoming listless, and even nervous. Horses are gluttons when it comes to oats, so keep your storage bin or barrel well out of the animal's

55

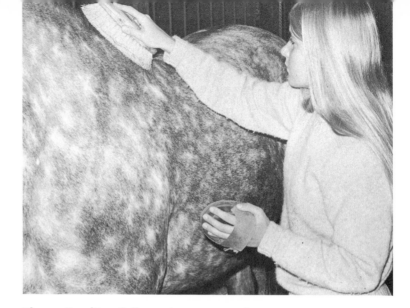

**Above: Brushing follows the curry comb treatment.
Below: Run a brush over a curry comb to free it of accumulated dirt.**

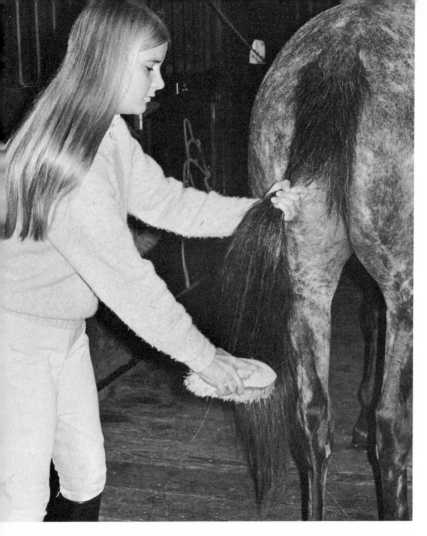

Use a mane comb or stiff bristled brush on the horse's tail.

reach. It is a fact that some horses have eaten themselves to death on oats. Wheat bran and corn—right on the cob—should be added to the horse's diet occasionally. Simply substitute a quart of bran for a quart of oats. Water should be available to the horse at all times.

Most owners establish a two-feedings-a-day routine. But never feed a horse after a vigorous ride, that is, when he is overheated. Allow him to cool off. Otherwise, he can become a victim of colic, a severe abdominal pain caused by gas pressure. It can be fatal. One rule of thumb says that you should treat a horse as you would yourself, and you won't go wrong. You would never eat right after a period of strenuous exercise; neither should your horse.

Even the healthiest horses become ill once in a while. You should know a good veterinarian who can be called in the case of a serious ailment or emergency. As you become better acquainted with your horse, you will learn to perceive certain signs that indicate all is not quite right. A dull coat, a lack of spirit, the failure to eat all his oats—any one of these may indicate that something is amiss. Familiarize yourself with the various afflictions that can beset a horse and maintain a well-stocked medicine cabinet. Alcohol, colic medicine, tincture of iodine, Vaseline, witch hazel, yellow oxide of mercury, rubbing liniment, lanolin, absorbent cotton, and bandaging are among the items it may contain. If you have a healthy horse, the only specialized treatment he requires is worming once a year, plus shoeing. Your horse should be shod every six weeks or so if you use him every day.

Your stable routine should include a regular time each day for grooming your horse. Doing it daily is important.

Start with the curry comb, an oval brush-type tool with metal or rubber teeth arranged in circular rows. Its purpose is to remove dirt or loose hair. The rubber curry comb is best. Begin on the horse's left side, using the comb with brisk, circular strokes on the horse's neck and body, but not on any sensitive areas, like the face or lower legs. You can use the body brush on these parts.

After the curry comb, use the stiff-bristled *dandy*

Most owners establish a two-feedings-a-day schedule.

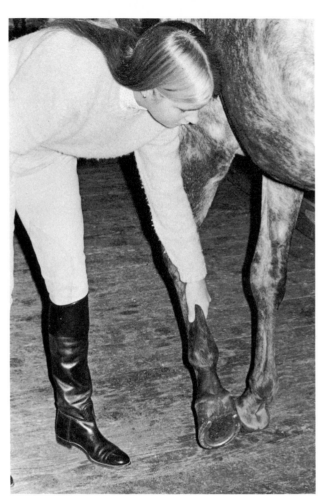

To raise a horse's hoof, slide your hand down his lower leg toward the hoof. Then simply lift.

In using the hoof pick, work from the horse's heel toward his toe.

brush to remove any dirt the curry comb has missed. Last, use the soft *body brush,* the most important brush in producing a clean, shining coat. It gets all the dust off and the horse enjoys the rubdown. For a really dazzling sheen, finish the job by going over the horse with a soft rag, rubbing his coat in the same direction the hair lies.

Combs and brushes are useless if they become clogged with dirt or hair. Tap the curry comb on your heel occasionally to clean it. To free a brush of accumulated hair, run it over a curry comb.

To clean the horse's mane and tail and straighten tangled hair, use a mane comb or a stiff bristled brush. Don't stand directly behind the animal when combing or brushing his tail; keep a bit to the left. Don't worry about hurting the horse when you comb his mane and tail. There are no nerve endings in the roots of mane or tail hairs.

Last, do the hoofs. Dirt and manure become packed in the hollow of each one and must be removed with a metal, question mark-shaped instrument called a *hoof pick.* To raise a horse's hoof, stand beside him, facing his rear. Lean against his shoulder or flank to throw his weight onto the opposite leg. Slide your hand down the forepart of the horse's lower leg toward the hoof and pick up his foot.

When cleaning the hoof, work from the heel toward the toe. Let the foot down gently when you have finished.

Owning a horse and caring for him is no easy matter. It takes no small amount of money, a good portion of the owner's spare time, and demands a keen sense of responsibility as well. But the relationship that develops between horse and owner is invariably deep, warm, and enduring, and serves as more than ample reward for whatever amount of toil is involved.

TACKING UP

If you are fortunate enough to own a horse of your own, you can ride whenever the urge strikes, provided you know how to "tack up"—how to equip your mount with saddle and bridle.

Always work from the left side. Begin with the saddle pad or blanket. Place it well up on the horse's withers, then slide it back so that the front edge of the pad just covers the withers. If the saddle fits well, no pad may be necessary. Some Eastern saddle owners who specialize in saddle mounts look disapprovingly upon the use of a saddle pad.

Place the saddle on the pad, making sure it settles comfortable over the coutours of the horse's back. Notice how the saddle is arched beneath the the pommel. This is to keep the underside away from the horse's backbone. If it should rub against the bone, it is likely to cause a painful sore.

If you are not using a pad, place the saddle well up on the withers, and then slide it back into place. The idea is to smooth the horse's coat so there will be no discomfort underneath. Once the saddle is in place, check it on both sides to be sure that the girth and stirrup leathers are not twisted. Then, from the left side, fasten the girth. In should be made tight

**Top: When tacking up, begin with the saddle pad.
Bottom: Place the saddle on the pad; be sure it settles comfortably on the horse's back.**

59

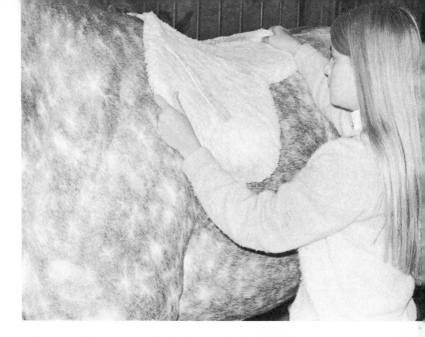

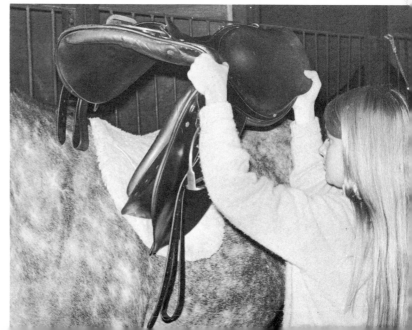

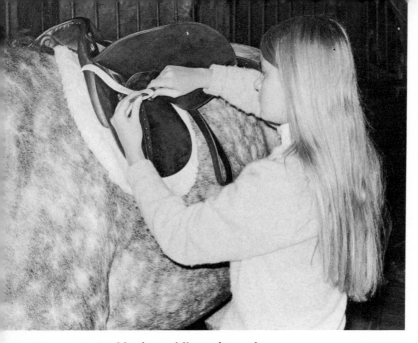

Buckle the saddle to the pad.

enough to enable you to stand in one stirrup without the saddle slipping, yet there should be room enough for you to squeeze your hand between the girth and the horse's stomach.

When you bridle the horse, again work from the left side. Pick up the bridle in your left hand by the crownpiece, the strap that goes over the horse's head behind the ears. With your right hand, drape the reins over the horse's neck. Make sure they are not twisted.

Once the reins are in place, switch the bridle to

60

your left hand, and raise the bit to the horse's mouth, passing his nose through the cheek straps. A horse will usually open his mouth when a bit is placed against his teeth. If yours doesn't, you can make him open by inserting your thumb and index finger into the gap on each side of the lower jaw where there are no teeth. These spaces are called bars. The bit should rest in these gaps, with the horse's tongue underneath it.

Once the bit is in his mouth, loop the crownpiece over his ears. Inspect the bridle carefully on each side to be sure there is no twisted harness. Adjust the browband and then buckle the throat latch. This passes over the horse's windpipe so it should be more loose than tight.

If your horse is wearing a Pelham, twist the curb chain so that it lies flat against his chin. It should be just loose enough to enable you to squeeze two fingers underneath without disturbing the bit.

If your horse has a tendency to hold his head high, or to raise his head when he feels the bit, he may require a martingale. Opinion is divided as to the value of the martingale, however, and you should get expert advice before you equip your horse with one. The standing martingale is the simplest type. It should be adjusted so that it does not impede

Opposite, left: Fasten the girth; don't make it too tight. Right: With your left hand, raise the bit to the horse's mouth, passing his nose through the cheekstraps.

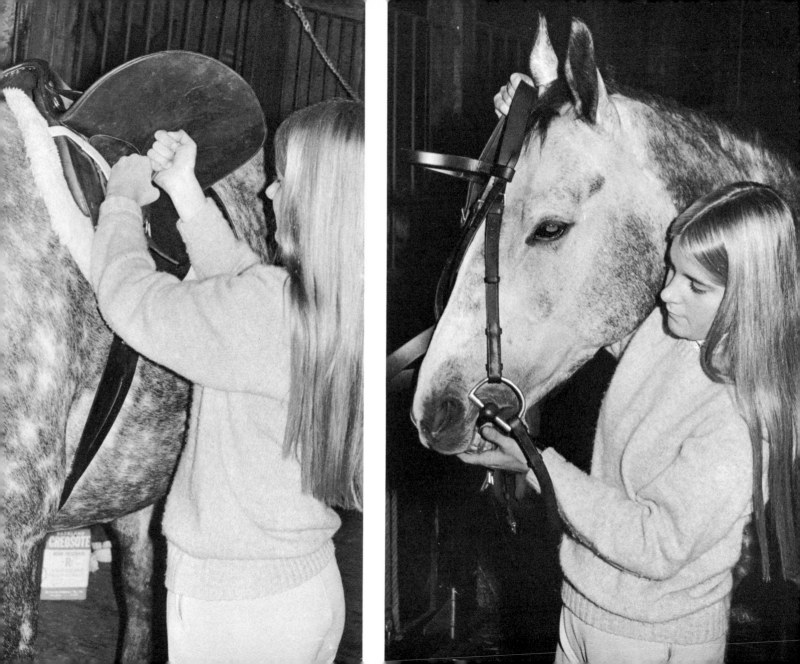

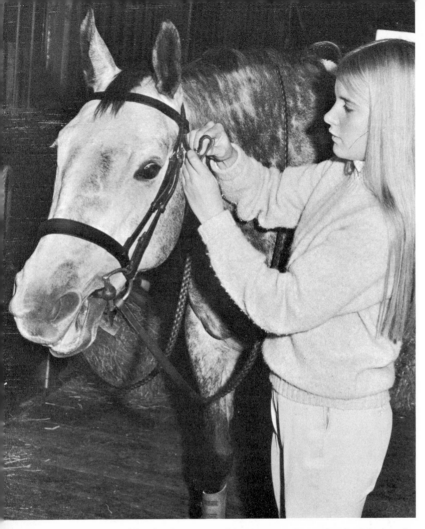

Buckle the harness, then inspect it on both sides to be sure it is not twisted.

the horse's freedom of action. The running martingale is used chiefly on jumpers.

If your horse is so built that the saddle tends to slip back, you will want to equip him with a breastplate. This is merely a piece of harness that crosses the horse's chest and is tied to the saddle, holding it in place.

After the ride, remove the bridle, then the saddle.

If your horse has a habit of holding his head high, he may require a martingale.

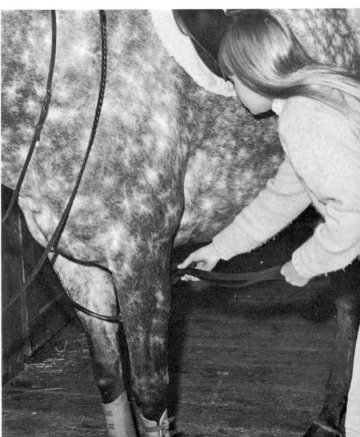

Drop the bit into a pail of water after you take it from the horse's mouth. Doing this will save you cleaning time later.

Be diligent about cleaning your tack. Use saddle soap and a damp sponge to clean the bridle leather. The soap must be worked into the leather to be effective.

Rub the horse down with a rag. If he is sweating heavily, go over him with a sweat scraper. Sponge off the saddle area, his nostrils, and mouth. Put a light blanket over him and walk him slowly until he is breathing normally. Do not feed or water him until he is cool.

Clean the saddle the same way, doing the underside first. It is extremely important to keep the saddle and all of its parts soft and flexible. Doing this not only helps to preserve the leather but, in addition, the leather grips the horse's back better when it's pliable and is much less likely to cause chafing or sores.

GLOSSARY

AMERICAN SADDLE HORSE—A breed of horses, raised originally in the United States, noted for a high-stepping gait.

APPALOOSA—A breed of horses developed in the West whose coat bears distinctive spotting.

BARS—The gaps on either side of the horse's lower jaw in which the bit rests.

BILLETS—Saddle straps to which the girth is attached.

BIT—The mouthpiece of the bridle.

BLAZE—A broad band of white extending down the front of the horse's face.

BODY BRUSH—A soft-bristled brush used to produce a sheen on the horse's coat.

BREASTPLATE—A part of the harness that runs across the horse's chest; used to keep the saddle from slipping to the rear.

BRIDLE—The leather head harness which supports the bit in the horse's mouth and, in combination with the reins, is used to guide the horse.

CANTER—An easy gallop; a three-beat gait.

CANTLE—The hind part of the saddle, usually curved upward.

COLIC—A malady common to horses; characterized by severe abdominal pain.

COLT—A male horse under the age of four.

CURRY COMB—An oval brush-type tool with metal or rubber teeth; used for removing dirt or loose hair from the horse's coat.

DANDY BRUSH—A stiff-bristled brush used in grooming the horse.

FILLY—A female horse under the age of four.

GAIT—Any of the ways in which a horse moves—a walk, trot, canter, etc.

GALLOP—The horse's fastest gait.

GELDING—A castrated male horse.

GIRTH—The band that passes underneath the horse to hold the saddle in place.

HAND—A unit of measure equal to four inches used in determining the height of a horse.

HEADSTALL—The part of the bridle that fits about the horse's head.

HOOF PICK—A small, metal question mark-shaped tool used for cleaning out a horse's hoofs.

MARE—A female horse over the age of four.

MARTINGALE—A piece of restraining harness worn by some horses.

PALOMINO—A type of horse, usually of Quarter Horse stock, characterized by his golden color and flaxen mane and tail.

PELHAM—A single-bar bit that features a curb chain which fastens under the horse's jaw and to which a second set of reins are attached.

PINTO—A horse with a mottled or spotted coat.

POMMEL—The front part of the saddle that curves upward.

QUARTER HORSE—A breed of horses developed in the United States primarily for short distance racing, usually a quarter of a mile.

REINS—Narrow leather straps attached to either side of the bit and held by the rider to control the horse.

RUNNING MARTINGALE—A strap that fastens to the girth, passes between the forelegs, through the neck strap, and divides into two branches, each of which ends in a ring through which the reins pass; used to hold down the horse's head.

SNAFFLE—A type of bit, jointed in the middle, with a large metal ring at each end. The reins are attached to the rings.

SNIP—A white mark at or between the horse's nostrils.

STANDARDBRED—A breed of trotting and pacing horses.

STANDING MARTINGALE—A strap that fastens to the girth, passes between the forelegs, through a loop in the neck strap, and fastens to the noseband; used to prevent the horse from holding his head too high.

STAR—A patch of white on the horse's forehead.

STOCKING—The white leg of a horse.

THOROUGHBRED—The breed of horse to to which all racing horses belong.

TREE—The frame of wood on which the saddle is constructed.

WITHERS—The highest part of the horse's back, at the base of the neck.

798
Sul

3169
(4up)

798
Sul   Sulli
              B

Date Due

APR
SEP